First published in the UK 2008 by
A & C Black Publishing Ltd
38 Soho Square
London
W1D 3HB
www.acblack.com

Copyright © 2008 Blake Publishing
Published 2007 by Black Education Pty Ltd, Australia

ISBN: 978-1-4081-0509-2

A CIP catalogue record for this book is available from the British Library.

Written by Lisa Thompson and Elizabeth Dowen
Publisher: Katy Pike
Series Editor: Eve Tonelli
Cover Design: Terry Woodley
Designer: Matt Lin
Printed in China by South China Printing Co. Ltd.

Cover image © moodboard/Corbis

Illustration credits: p19 (br) (aap); p9 (bl), p13 (middle), p18 (br), p24 (tl),
p24 (br) - Shutterstock

This book is produced using paper made from wood grown in managed,
sustainable forests. It is natural, renewable and recyclable. The logging and
manufacturing processes conform to the environmental regulations of the
country of origin.

All the Internet addresses given in this book were correct at the time of
going to press. The author and publishers regret any inconvenience caused
if addresses have changed or sites have ceased to exist, but can accept no
responsibility for any such changes.

WHAT'S IT LIKE TO BE A...?

CHEF

Elizabeth Dowen   Lisa Thompson

Contents

The Crooked Spoon Secret Dessert

Get the buttery flavour to match the tartness of the berries.

Be careful with the sugar!

Try lining the pastry with some crushed ginger biscuits — should complement the fruit nicely.

Ingredients

Part A

450 grams berries (strawberries, blueberries, raspberries and blackberries)

? icing sugar

zest of 1 lemon

mascarpone cream

2 ginger biscuits, crushed

I wish I could remember how much sugar to use!

Part B

500g plain flour

1 teaspoon salt

1 tablespoon white sugar

1 cup unsalted butter, chilled and cut into small pieces

ice water

DID YOU KNOW?

Did you know that early American colonists made grey paint by boiling blueberries in milk?

Recipe

Dish: <u>Secret Dessert</u> Serves: <u>four</u>

Divide pastry into four equal portions.
On a lightly floured surface, roll each portion into a
20 cm circle. Place the four pastry circles into
scalloped baking tins and place in the fridge for one hour.
Bake pastry in moderate oven for
15 minutes until golden. Cool.
Spoon a layer of mascarpone into the pastry.
Combine the berries, and zest in a large bowl.
Heap berry mixture on top of mascarpone.
Lightly dust with icing sugar and serve.

shopping list

thyme
basil
carrots
tomatoes
onions
shiitake mushrooms
garlic
butter
cream
cumin
ginger

DID YOU KNOW?

THE STRAWBERRY AND LOVE
Because of its heart shape and red colour, the strawberry was the symbol of Venus, the Roman goddess of love.

Love at first bite!

5

PREPARATION AT
The Crooked Spoon

Preparation begins

"Where are the carrots I ordered, and the herbs? Where are those herbs? Can someone find out what's happened to our meat delivery? It should have been here by now ..."

It's early in the day and the deliveries have begun to arrive. The fruit and vegetable orders are checked off, Matt chases up the meat order, and our seafood delivery — fresh off the boat — is expected any minute. Only the finest ingredients are acceptable in my restaurant.

The Crooked Spoon's kitchen is getting ready for lunch service. This is prep time, and the kitchen is busy but calm. Stock pots are simmering, watched over by James, my apprentice. Food is prepared and seasoned. Sauces are stirred.

asparagus, for one of the entreés

Preparation, preparation!

We need lots of potatoes!

The mood changes once service begins, because people sitting down to eat don't want to wait too long for their food. If we're busy it can quickly become a high pressure environment, where timing is everything. Being a chef is hard work with long hours, but it is also a very rewarding career.

Yummy cheese, perfect for the platter!

Today is more hectic than usual — and also more exciting! Tonight's dinner service will be special. I have been preparing for this night for weeks — writing and rewriting menus, testing and tweaking recipes, tossing around new ideas and retrying old favourites.

A very special person will be dining in my restaurant tonight — the person who introduced me to cooking.

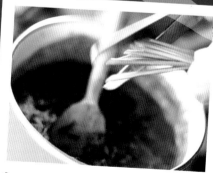
Fresh seafood, makes my bisque!

Chives — one of my favourite herbs!

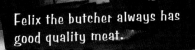
Felix the butcher always has good quality meat.

My love of cooking

A welcoming smile is staff policy at The Crooked Spoon!

When I was a boy, I was always in and out of my grandma's kitchen. I would catch the smells of what was in the oven or on the stove, and I learnt to predict what delicious treats were coming my way.

My grandmother introduced me to the magic of food. She would make me taste her cooking with my eyes closed, and I would try to guess the ingredients she had used. Together, we would make up recipes and experiment with different combinations of ingredients.

But there was always one dish that baffled me — a delicious dessert that remained a secret because I never unlocked the combination of flavours. It seemed like a simple dish to make, but getting the flavours to balance was not easy.

Grandma showed me how much fun cooking could be. At the weekend, early in the morning, we would visit the markets. We tasted and smelled foods from all over the world. For my birthday each year, grandma took me to a restaurant. I began to understand the possibilities of food and cooking, and I met the people who worked with food as a career.

When I finished school I did a four-year apprenticeship to become a chef. Then I travelled the world, working in lots of different kitchens, before finally returning home and opening my own restaurant — The Crooked Spoon. The restaurant is named after the tasting spoon my grandma gave me as a boy.

Tonight, Grandma is my special guest at The Crooked Spoon – along with the rest of my family. We are celebrating her eightieth birthday, and I am going to make her the secret dessert!

DID YOU KNOW?

Honey forever

Honey is the only food that doesn't spoil. Honey found in the tombs of ancient Egyptian pharaohs was tested and found to be edible — even after thousands of years in storage!

BECOMING A CHEF

Hospitality and catering is one of the largest industries in Britain. There is currently a shortage of chefs and the industry is growing. You could be employed in:

- a hotel, restaurant, pub, café or fast-food outlet
- a holiday centre or conference venue
- a hospital or a company's staff canteen/restaurant
- a school, college or university
- the Armed Forces.

You can learn to cook on the job, but it takes time, commitment and specialist training to learn the more professional skills of cooking.

There are various ways of getting started. For fast food or simple meals, training is usually provided on the job. But for quality catering and training

as a chef, formal training and recognised qualifications are very important. It is possible to specialise in a particular area while training.

Most chefs complete a very demanding apprenticeship. They learn about and practise

food preparation, cooking and presentation.

A chef must be able to plan menus, order ingredients, and prepare, season and cook a wide variety of foods. Chefs also supervise kitchen staff and maintain strict levels of cleanliness and hygiene in the kitchen.

Trainee cooks and chefs may start work after leaving school or after a full-time college course. Most hotels and restaurants, depending on their size, employ one or more trained chefs who prepare all the meals, with help from kitchen assistants. There are no specific educational entry requirements for a career as a cook or chef, although individual employers may set their own.

Cooking as a job is very different from cooking at home. In most types of professional cooking, you cook for large numbers of people, using different techniques and equipment from your own kitchen.

WANTED — 1 GOOD CHEF

To be a good chef you need:

- good health and stamina - you are on your feet all day
- good coordination — for working with sharp knives
- a good memory for details
- **the ability to work well under pressure and remain calm**
- to follow instructions carefully and work quickly and efficiently
- **good organisational skills**
- the ability to work on your own and as part of a team
- **attention to health and safety**

- A kitchen can be a hot, busy and dangerous place to work.

KEEP IN MIND THAT A CHEF WORKS LONG HOURS, OFTEN AT WEEKENDS AND DURING HOLIDAYS AND TIME OFF IS OFTEN WHEN OTHER PEOPLE ARE AT WORK! LOTS OF CHEFS WORK SPLIT SHIFTS - BEING ON DUTY MORE THAN ONCE A DAY, COVERING TWO MEAL-TIMES. HOWEVER, IN SOME JOBS (LIKE IN SCHOOL CANTEENS AND COMPANY RESTAURANTS) THE HOURS OF WORK ARE SHORTER.

WHO'S WHO IN THE KITCHEN?

Working in a kitchen is a team effort — every member has their own tasks and responsibilities. Team members must work together smoothly when a kitchen gets really busy. In a small kitchen, a team of two cooks do everything!

Chef de partie or section chef

These cooks are responsible for a part of the kitchen work, for example sauces, soups and some main courses. They could also be expected to prepare pastry (breads, sweets and patisserie), vegetables and larder foods (starters, cold meats, salads, dressings).

Kitchen Assistants

Kitchen assistants do the routine work of preparing vegetables, stacking dishwashers, scrubbing pans, weighing ingredients and keeping the kitchen clean. The job involves some simple cooking tasks too. You need to be quite strong, practical and clean and tidy. This is one way to begin a career as a chef, if you're prepared to gain qualifications while you work.

Commis Chef

The commis chef is also known as an assistant chef or chef-in-training. They spend a few months in each section of the kitchen learning all the different skills involved in the job of a chef.

Where there are several chefs working in a large kitchen, such as in a hotel, each chef will often specialise in the preparation of particular dishes or certain processes like making sauces or pastries.

Chef Sauciers
Prepare, season and cook sauces, and the meat and fish dishes they accompany. They also make soups and casseroles.

Chef Garde Mangers
Prepare and present salads, cold dishes and cold *hors d'oeuvres** and buffets.

**Hors d'oeuvre* (pronounced *ore-derv*): a small dish, usually savoury, served before the main meal.

Chef Entremetiers
Prepare, cook and present vegetables, pasta and egg dishes.

Chef Patissiers
Prepare, cook and present desserts and pastries, and may also make ice-creams and sorbets.

WHO'S IN CHARGE?

THE **HEAD CHEF** OR MAÎTRE DE CUISINE MANAGES THE KITCHEN AND MAY BE RESPONSIBLE FOR MORE THAN ONE KITCHEN. THEY:

A waiter must remember seating arrangements, carry dishes, answer questions about the food and take orders.

- create new recipes and menus
- oversee the production of meals
- hire staff
- advise staff on the size of servings and quality standards
- check the quality of ingredients an the dishes prepared with them
- estimate labour and food costs, and alter menus to stay within budget
- meet customers about menus for special occasions, such as weddings and parties
- arrange for equipment purchases ar repairs.
- make sure health and safety regulations are maintained

The Sous chef

(pronounced soo chef) is an assistant to the head chef. They must be skilled in all areas of kitchen work. They also:

- assist head chefs with menu planning
- demonstrate new techniques or equipment
- act as team leaders, managing and supervising staff
- deal with suppliers and control the costs
- oversee health and safety

A chef's hat is properly known as a **toque blanche** (French for white hat).

WHO'S WHO AT THE CROOKED SPOON? IN OUR MEDIUM-SIZED KITCHEN, THE TEAM CONSISTS OF:

- 1 head chef (that's me)
- 2 sous chefs
- 1 chef saucier
- 2 entrée chefs (to prepare first courses only)
- 3 kitchen assistants
- 1 kitchen hand.

A large restaurant has a *maître d'* (pronounced may-tra-dee), which is short for *maître d'hôtel*, meaning master of the house. This person takes reservations, assigns customers to tables and manages the waiting staff.

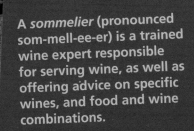

A *sommelier* (pronounced som-mell-ee-er) is a trained wine expert responsible for serving wine, as well as offering advice on specific wines, and food and wine combinations.

Moments in culinary history

1634
The town of Dijon in France is granted the exclusive right to make mustard.

1671
The Prince de Conde's cook dies by falling on his sword when not enough fish is delivered for a banquet honouring King Louis XIV. The missing fish arrives 15 minutes later.

the town of Dijon

1682
Champagne is invented by Dom Perignon, a blind monk and cellarman at Hautevilliers Abbey, France.

1740
Paolo Adami receives a licence to open the first pasta factory in Venice, Italy.

Champagne, très bonne!

1765
A new business in Paris begins to sell restorative soups. The shops are known as restaurants (from the French word *restaurer*, to restore).

Pasta comes in different shapes and colours.

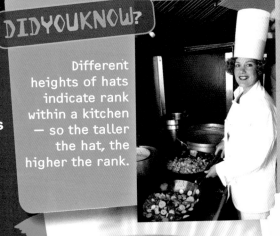

Different heights of hats indicate rank within a kitchen — so the taller the hat, the higher the rank.

1782

The first restaurant as we know them today — with a menu, tables, waiters and regular hours — opens in Paris. It is called the *Grande Taverne de Londres*.

1800

The scientist Count von Rumford develops the first commercially-available kitchen stove.

1820s

Chefs begin wearing large white hats, known as toques. A cooking tradition says that a chef's toque has 100 pleats to show the number of ways an egg can be cooked.

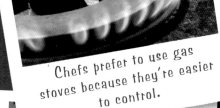

Chefs prefer to use gas stoves because they're easier to control.

1840

Gas stoves are first used.

1980

Restaurant owners in Marseilles, France, agree to prepare *bouillabaisse* (pronounced boo-yeh-bess), a traditional fish stew, only from certain ingredients and to a certain method.

The fish and shellfish in bouillabaisse is complemented with herbs and spices.

The Cordon Bleu is a famous French school of cooking. It was founded in Paris in 1895 by journalist Marthe Distel to teach French cuisine to the daughters of wealthy families. Today, it attracts amateur and professional cooks from around the world, and has schools in Australia, Mexico, the United Kingdom, Canada, Korea and Japan. The term cordon bleu comes from the sky-blue ribbons worn by a group of French knights renowned for their extravagant and luxurious banquets.

FAMOUS CHEFS

Marc-Antoine Careme (1784–1833)

"The king of cooks and the cook for Kings."

Black caviar and toast. The best caviar comes from sturgeon fish in the Caspian Sea.

Careme was considered the master of French cooking, creating dishes that often looked more like sculptures. He cooked for royalty and the rich and famous. His cuisine was the talk of Europe.

Careme travelled and discovered different foods and eating habits. He introduced to France such delicacies as caviar (unfertilised fish eggs) and *paskha* (a creamy Russian cheesecake).

While in England, he produced a jellied custard set in a crown of ladyfingers (long, thin biscuits). He named it the Charlotte Russe

— a pastry still baked today. Careme also prepared massive feasts. At one military festival, he served 10,000 guests from a menu that required 6 cows, 75 calves, 250 sheep, 8,000 turkeys, 2,000 chickens, 1,000 partridges, 500 hams and 2,000 fish.

Careme was also a spy! He relayed information he overheard at dinner tables all over Europe back to France.

FAMILY SAUCES

Careme classified cooking sauces into four families, each of which was based on a mother sauce:

- *allemande* (pronounced alla-marnd), based on stock with egg yolk and lemon juice
- *béchamel* (pronounced be-shem-el), based on flour and milk
- **espagnole** (pronounced espa-nol), based on brown stock and beef
- *velouté* (pronounced ve-loot-ay), based on a light broth of fish, chicken or veal.

Jamie Oliver (born 1975)

"From quite an early age I realised the effect that good food can have on others."

Oliver is a British celebrity chef who became popular through a TV cooking show called *The Naked Chef*.

From the age of eight, Oliver started helping in the kitchen of his parent's pub. Jamie left school at 16 to attend a catering college. After college, he travelled to France to learn more about cooking. He was asked to make *The Naked Chef* while working in London as a sous chef.

Jamie Oliver is known for his simple recipes made from fresh ingredients. His cooking shows have been shown in 50 countries, and his cookbooks have sold millions of copies.

You may have heard of Fifteen. These are Jamie's restaurants, based in Cornwall and central London. They offer training to young, unemployed people. Find out more at: www.fifteen.net.

Being a celebrity chef is very hard work!

A world of
FLAVOURS

Every country has flavours and ingredients that make its cuisine unique. Chefs love to try different foods from around the world, and incorporate new ideas and flavours in their own cooking.

England — bacon, mustard, oats, potatoes, Worcestershire sauce

RICE IS NICE

Rice is the staple food — the main part of the diet — for more than half of the world's population.

Ireland — cabbage, oats, oysters, potatoes

Mexico — chilli, corn, lime, chocolate

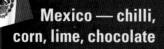

Argentina — beef, pasta, fish, corn

Libya — couscous, lamb, lemon, coriander, onions, olive oil

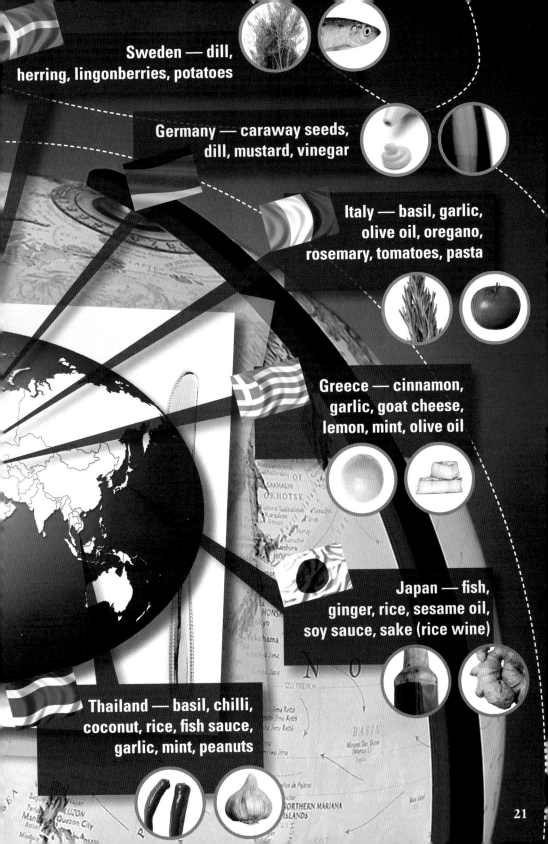

Sweden — dill, herring, lingonberries, potatoes

Germany — caraway seeds, dill, mustard, vinegar

Italy — basil, garlic, olive oil, oregano, rosemary, tomatoes, pasta

Greece — cinnamon, garlic, goat cheese, lemon, mint, olive oil

Japan — fish, ginger, rice, sesame oil, soy sauce, sake (rice wine)

Thailand — basil, chilli, coconut, rice, fish sauce, garlic, mint, peanuts

Cuisine from around the world
....

Enjoy this selection from the world's diverse food traditions.

Kim chee, Korea
Fermented cabbage soaked in salt and red chili. It is usually left for several weeks before serving, but can be stored for months in clay pots buried underground.

Hakarl, Iceland
Shark that has been killed, buried in gravel by the ocean for months, dug up, washed, and hung to dry.

Fugu, Japan
The meat of the poisonous puffer fish. Only specially licensed chefs are allowed to prepare fugu — even so, several people die each year from fugu poisoning.

Water bugs, Thailand
Like giant cockroaches but with a harder shell.

Fois gras (fattened liver of a duck or goose) and truffles (a fungus).

Black pudding and apples. Blood is the main ingredient in black pudding.

Other specials currently not on the menu >>

Tripe, made from the stomach lining of cows or sheep.

Jellied cow's foot, *Poland*
Chopped cow's foot cooked for several hours with spices, garlic, salt and pepper. It sets in the refrigerator with a jelly-like layer of fat over the top, and is usually served with horseradish.

Blood dumplings, *Sweden*
Flour, reindeer blood and salt dumplings, served with bacon, butter and lingonberry jam.

Seal flipper pie, *Canada*
Fresh seal flippers, pork fat, onions and Worcestershire sauce, baked in a pastry-covered pie.

snails

Feeling REALLY hungry?

For possibly the largest dish on any menu, try whole roasted camel, sometimes served at Bedouin wedding feasts. It's a roast camel stuffed with a sheep's carcass, which is stuffed with a chicken, which is stuffed with fish, which is stuffed with eggs. Any gaps are stuffed with rice and nuts.

CHEF SENSE : TONGUE AND NOSE

bitter sour

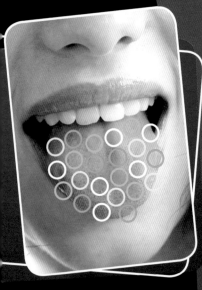

salty sweet

A chef needs to have a highly developed sense of smell and an understanding of flavour and texture. The tongue has different types of nerve endings called tastebuds that detect the four basic flavours — sour, salty, bitter and sweet.

People once thought that different areas of the tongue detected different tastes — sour tastes on the sides, sweet tastes at the front, bitter tastes at the back, and salty tastes detected all over of the tongue.

Now, it is known that there are only small differences in sensitivity across the tongue, and sweet, sour, salty and bitter are tasted all over the tongue.

Your nose lets you know the difference between burnt toast, roast lamb and chocolate cake. It does this with help from body parts deep inside yournasal cavity and head. On the roof of the nasal cavity (the space behind your nose) is the olfactory epithelium, which

contains special receptors sensitive to odour molecules. These receptors are very small — there are at least 10 million of them in your nose!

There are hundreds of different types of odour receptors, each with the ability to sense certain molecules. When the odour receptors are stimulated, signals travel along the olfactory nerve to the brain. The brain interprets the combination of odour molecules to recognise any one of about 10,000 different smells.

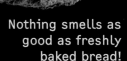

Nothing smells as good as freshly baked bread!

SPECIAL POWERS

There can be large differences in our ability to taste. People with a very sensitive sense of taste are called supertasters — they find vegetables bitter, particularly brussel sprouts.

SMELL-LESS-NESS

Your sense of smell declines from about the age of 40.

Test your nosey food critic

The ability to smell and taste go together, because odours from foods allow us to taste more fully. Try this simple experiment. Take a bite of any food and think about how it tastes. Then, pinch and hold your nose and take another bite. Notice the difference?

TO YOUR STATIONS

All kitchens — no matter how large or small — can be divided into five basic areas: storage, preparation, cooking, washing and serving.

A kitchen is designed like a factory — raw materials (ingredients) come in at one end of the production line and exit at the other end as a meal ready to be served.

Kitchens are divided into clearly defined areas, called stations, that handle different tasks. Because a kitchen is a busy and sometimes dangerous environment, it is organised to make it easy to work in and move around. For example, waiting staff and kitchen staff meet where dishes are served and dirty plates collected, but otherwise keep out of each other's way.

shelves for storage

access to dining room

microwave oven

stove top and grill

DID YOU KNOW?

Chocolate love!
Eating chocolate releases feel-good chemicals in the brain. That's why we come back for more. Chocolate also contains a natural substance meant to have the same effect on the body as falling in love!

LOVE

JUST LIKE HOME?

Although a commercial kitchen in a restaurant has the same purpose as your kitchen at home, most things in a commercial kitchen are bigger.

While you may have a dishwasher at home, a commercial kitchen might have two or three. Rather than just a fridge, a commercial kitchen might have a walk-in cool room.

A commercial kitchen has more than one oven, and large, heavy-duty stoves. A restaurant kitchen also has strong air extractors for removing hot, dirty air from the kitchen.

air extractor

ladles

benchtops for food preparation

chopping boards

oven

CARVING UP THE KITCHEN

Every chef has a set of knives. Although there are many different types of knives, a chef's set usually includes:

- chopping knife for cutting meat
- cleaver
- large chopping or preparation knife for vegetables
- filleting knife for fish
- boning knife
- paring knife for delicate cutting
- carving or bread knife
- serrated knife
- sharpening stone and stick.

A knife block protects blades when not in use.

Different nozzles for the piping bag produce different decorative patterns.

Depending on a chef's area of expertise, they may use special preparation utensils.

- whisk, for whipping together ingredients such as eggs, cream and milk
- zester, for removing zest (thin pieces of skin) from citrus fruit, such as lemons, limes and oranges
- mandoline slicer, for making very thin and patterned slices of vegetables
- moulds and piping bags for desserts

Preparing salmon in a Japanese restaurant.

SUSHi SLiCERS

Sushi is a Japanese dish traditionally made with rice and either vegetables or seafood, with egg occasionally added. Raw fish is a key ingredient.

Sushi chefs use special knives to prepare their dishes, including knives designed to cut particular species of fish. For example, the *fugu hiki* is specifically designed to fillet the puffer fish (*fugu*), and the *unagisaki hocho* is designed for filleting eel. For preparing very large fish, such as large tuna, a knife over a metre long may be used.

Unlike most knives, sushi knives are sharpened on only one edge — so there are different knives for right-handed and left-handed chefs!

sushi

whisk

grater

vegetable peeler

pizza cutter

mortar and pestle

juicer

ladle

29

ALL IN A DAY'S WORK AT

Part 1

The Crooked Spoon

I wake up thinking about the specials we can prepare for lunch and dinner at The Crooked Spoon. To keep the menu fresh, specials are new dishes that are created from the latest fresh produce.

10 am — I arrive at the restaurant and check the deliveries for quality and accuracy — I ensure we received what we ordered. Matthew, one of my kitchen assistants, is already storing the deliveries.

eschallots for cooking, radishes for a special sauce

I make sure the kitchen was cleaned thoroughly after last night's work. This lets me know that my staff are keeping up with their responsibilities.

10:30 am — I check that the cool rooms and storerooms are tidy, and that stock levels are sufficient. I look at the reservations list for lunch and dinner to get a feel for how busy the day will be.

10:45 am — The other chefs begin to arrive. I run through the menu with the sous chefs, and discuss the specials that I have in mind.

Time to get started!

I ask Fiona, one of the sous chefs, to suggest and prepare specials for tomorrow's dinner menu. She will present them for tasting by the staff tomorrow afternoon.

11 am — Each chef prepares their station — their work area — and they begin seasoning, chopping and saucing.

Chop, chop, so much to cut!

12 noon — The Crooked Spoon is now open for lunch! When the first order is taken — for the Warm Pork and Asparagus Spinach Salad — I call it out loudly. Calling the orders sounds chaotic when the kitchen is really busy, but it keeps the staff focused, so they can concentrate on cooking, presentation and timing.

Before every dish leaves the kitchen, I check that the presentation meets my standards, and that it was prepared in a reasonable amount of time — I don't want my customers to wait too long for their meals!

3 pm — The kitchen closes for lunch and everything is cleaned and packed away. Food stocks are checked and new orders phoned to suppliers.

The staff take a well-deserved break before The Crooked Spoon re-opens for dinner, and my special guest arrives.

sautéed pork for the salad

Asparagus spears — delicious!

Fresh, crusty loaves — smell good!

We make and bake our own bread.

The kitchen gets frantic!

COOKING 101

Basic methods of cooking

- baking — cooking by dry heat in the oven
- roasting — cooking by high-heat baking (usually with some fat added)
- broiling — cooking at a high temperature with an overhead heat source
- grilling — cooking under an open heat element
- frying — cooking in a pan with a moderate amount of fat at a moderate temperature, or deep-fried while submerged in oil at a high temperature
- boiling — cooking in boiling liquid
- simmering — cooking in liquid below boiling point
- sauté — cooking in a pan quickly in a small amount of fat at a high temperature
- steaming — cooking food by exposing it directly to steam
- braising — browning food in a little fat, then slowly cooking in a covered pot with a little liquid at a low temperature

sautéed mushro⟨

For soft yolks, boil eggs three minutes; for hard yolks boil for ten.

steamed dumplings

The next frontier

It is part of a chef's job to unlock the wonderful secrets that food holds — how certain ingredients taste when combined with others, how foods react to different kinds of cooking, and how ingredients can be treated and prepared. Great chefs are always pushing the boundaries of what food can taste and look like.

Most chefs cannot work without butter and oil, garlic, salt and herbs.

← Asian dishes are often cooked using bamboo steamers.

DID YOU KNOW?

A brief history of the potato!

Spanish explorers brought the potato from Central America to Europe in the 1500s. At first, the potato was mistrusted and considered un-Christian as there is no mention of it in the Bible. This prevented it gaining widespread acceptance, but slowly it was promoted as a medicinal plant. The potato became popular during times of war as it lay underground and avoided destruction.

Lamb being trussed — bound with string to hold it together — before roasting.

STOCK UP

Possibly a chef's best friend is stock — the liquid in which meat, fish or vegetables are simmered for long periods. A stock is the basis of most sauces and soups.

Works of ART

Good cooking tastes great — and it looks great. Part of the enjoyment of eating a meal prepared by a chef is the way the food is presented.

How would you present a cooked whole fish? With or without the eyes? How would you include a mushroom sauce with a steak dish? Poured over the meat or next to it on the plate? The presentation of a dish is one way that chefs add personal style to their work and create culinary works of art.

A garnish is a decoration that adds to the presentation of a dish. A simple rule of garnishing is to use ingredients in the dish itself to decorate the plate. This is the easiest and most sensible way to garnish, because you know the tastes will blend.

DIDYOUKNOW?

If you want to cook in the top hotels and restaurants, and perhaps be a famous chef yourself one day, you should try to get experience at the best establishments from an early stage. Look for basic jobs with training in four- or five-star hotels or restaurants which are highly rated by the various guides and food critics. That's how chefs like Gordon Ramsay and Jamie Oliver got started.

PLATE UP

The way a dish is assembled on a plate is called plating. Here are the golden rules of plating.

1. Don't overcrowd a plate with food — leave one-third (or sometimes more) of the plate empty.
2. Odd numbers of food items on a plate generally look better than even numbers.
3. Put food on the plate — no matter what its temperature — immediately before serving it.
4. If serving hot food, make sure that the food and the plate are hot when plating.
5. Make sure plate edges are clean. If you need to clean them, use a moist paper towel in one circular sweep.

Art as food, food as art.

Garnish ideas

Chives on a smoked trout omelette
Whole, mixed (black and green) peppercorns on marinated fresh anchovies
Ground salt sprinkled on a steak

Hot tip

The colour of a chilli is no indication of its spiciness — but size usually is. The smaller the chilli, the hotter it is. The hottest chilli in the world is the *habanero*.

MEASURING UP

The measuring system used for cooking varies depending on where you are. In England, most recipes use the metric measuring system. Some countries use a system that includes cups and spoons - it all depends on what country you are cooking in!

Basic measurements a chef must know

1 teaspoon (t or tsp.) = 5 millilitres

1 dessertspoon (D) = 2 teaspoons = 10 millilitres

1 tablespoon (T or tbsp.) = 3 teaspoons = 15 millilitres

1 cup (c) = 250 millilitres

2 cups = 500 millilitres

4 cups = 1 litre

measuring spoons

kitchen timer

kitchen scales

baking tray

measuring jug

HEAPED OR EVEN?

Some recipes have extra instructions for measuring the correct amount of an ingredient. Here's how to measure out what the recipe wants:

Firmly packed — press the ingredient tightly into the measuring device

Lightly packed — press the ingredient lightly into the measuring device

Even/level — level the top of the measuring device with a spatula or knife, so that it is flat and even with the rim

Rounded — allow the ingredient to pile up above the rim of the measuring device

Heaping/heaped — measure as much of the ingredient as the measuring device will hold

Level or firmly packed?

levelling off the flour

Preheat the oven to avoid burning your hard work!

WHY IS IT IMPORTANT TO PREHEAT?

As an oven heats up, it puts out extra heat to reach the selected temperature. If you put food in the oven before it has reached the desired temperature it could burn. Preheating an oven usually takes 5–10 minutes.

Prospects and pay

For staff with good training and experience, there are opportunities to work in posts of responsibility, to move from one sector of the industry to another and to work abroad. It is an industry with lots of scope for broadening your experience and developing your career. Although a kitchen assistant may earn little over the minimum wage, a head chef can earn £25,000+.

WORLD FAMOUS
DISHES

Some dishes have become so popular that they are made over

and over again. A famous dish that identifies a chef

is known as a signature dish.

Peach Melba

This dessert was created for Australian opera singer, Dame Nellie Melba, by the great French chef, Auguste Escoffier, in 1893. Kaiser Wilhelm II once told Escoffier, "I am the Emperor of Germany, but you are the Emperor of chefs."

500g fresh raspberries
2 tbsp icing sugar
juice of 2 lemons
8 fresh peaches, peeled and sliced
8 scoops vanilla ice-cream

In a saucepan, bring peaches, raspberries, sugar and lemon juice to a boil. Reduce heat and simmer for five minutes. Chill, if desired, and serve over ice-cream. Serves eight people.

Waldorf Salad

A salad created by Oscar Tschirky — known as Oscar of the Waldorf — for the opening of the Waldorf Hotel in New York in 1893. (Oscar didn't use walnuts originally.)

2-3 sticks of celery, cubed
2 apples, peeled and cubed
walnuts, chopped
1 lettuce, washed and dried
juice of 1 lemon
5-6 tablespoons of mayonnaise
salt and freshly ground pepper

Toss apples with lemon juice. Add remaining ingredients and mix well. Serves four people.

Sachertorte

Possibly the world's most famous chocolate cake, invented by 16-year-old apprentice cook, Franz Sasher, in 1832 in Vienna, Austria. The original recipe is a well-kept secret.

130 grams butter
110 grams icing sugar
6 egg yolks
130 grams chocolate, melted
130 grams flour
6 egg whites
100 grams fine granulated sugar
apricot jam

Beat together the butter and icing sugar. Gradually add in the egg yolks and the melted chocolate, stirring constantly. Beat the egg whites with the granulated sugar to stiff peaks, and mix them into the chocolate batter. Gently fold in the flour.

Place the mixture in a buttered mould and bake for 60 minutes at 180° Celsius. Let cool, remove from the mould, slice through the middle horizontally and fill with a layer of apricot jam. Glaze with chocolate. Serves eight people.

SAFETY FIRST

Always point saucepan handles away from the edge of the stove, and open the lids of steaming pots away from you.

The Crooked Spoon

Part 2: The Secret Dessert

Back at The Crooked Spoon

4:30 pm — While the staff are on their break, I work on the secret recipe — my special dessert for Gran tonight. The berries are wonderfully juicy and fresh, but I must get their sweetness to balance with the pastry.

The staff returns and we prepare for the dinner service.

We all sit down to taste samples of the specials and run through the ingredients — our customers are sure to ask questions about what is in the dishes and how they are prepared.

6 pm — The Crooked Spoon opens again and diners begin to arrive. We're ready and waiting for the first order.

6:15 pm — The first order is in. I receive the docket and begin delegating to the different chefs and sections to prepare. The cooking is underway.

7:20 pm — The order from my family's table reaches the kitchen. She has ordered a beetroot and herb risotto as a first course, followed by the pan-fried rabbit and warm apple salad. Great choice! I choose to cook my grandma's main dish myself.

Look at the beautiful berries — it's going to be great!

the pastry cup, ready for the fruit mixture

It's getting busy now.

7:25 pm — Suddenly there is a loud crash from the cool room — a container of broccoli has fallen onto some pastry cups that were ready for one of the dessert dishes. There is no time to make more pastry cups, so that dish will have to come off the menu.

7:50 pm — One of the waiting staff tells me that he has lost an order, and a couple have been waiting for 40 minutes for their meals. I am not happy! Producing these dishes becomes my first priority.

I entrust my best sous chef with completing Gran's dishes.

Cut quickly, but be careful!

pasta on the boil

Even though it's frantic, you have to stay in control.

Got to peel the prawns quickly!

The kitchen hots up!

ALL IN A DAY'S WORK AT

The Crooked Spoon

Part 2: The Secret Dessert

8 pm — The kitchen is hot, alive and buzzing with activity. Orders are called out — "another chicken, three beef, a pasta on 12". Side dishes are called for. Sauces are poured. Garnish containers need to be restocked. Pots and pans are being shuffled over flames, and from front burners to back burners. Every station is a flurry of activity and a blur of hands.

9:10 pm — The pace is slowing now and I switch my attention to the dessert. She hasn't ordered a dessert so my creation will be a surprise. I've decided to keep its presentation very simple — positioned alone on a simple white plate. I watch nervously as the waiter weaves out through the dining room to Gran's table with the dessert.

Peering through the kitchen door, I see the look of surprise and (I hope!) delight on her face.

I hold my breath. Then Gran cries aloud towards the kitchen, "Alistair — you've done it! You have unlocked the tastes in our special dessert, and it is DELICIOUS."

The other diners in the restaurant begin to look back and forth — and then we are bombarded with orders for The Crooked Spoon Secret Dessert!

The stove's on fire tonight!

Have to cook the same thing three times.

Grandma's secret dessert

OPPORTUNITIES FOR CHEFS

In the hospitality industry there is always the opportunity to work in another country. This is all part of widening your experience of different ingredients and styles of cooking.

- You could start your own business — a restaurant, café or catering company.

- Your skills as a chef could be used in costumer services (hotels, motels, bed-and-breakfasts), food and beverage businesses (cafés, restaurants), tourism-related services (cooking for airlines and cruise ships) and the conference and events industries.

- You may choose to specialise in a particular type of cuisine, such as seafood, vegetarian or modern British or French cuisine.

- Finally, a chef gets the chance to build close relationships with a kitchen team — and often gets free meals at work!

DIDYOUKNOW?

The Applied Ability Awards (Triple A's) have been developed by a number of professional culinary organisations led by the British Food Trust. Certificates are awarded at two levels, Foundation Chef and Chef, following practical exams and are generally aimed at people already working in the industry. The scheme is still in a trial period and will be more widely available via employers from November 2008.

Apprenticeships in hospitality and catering offer training with an employer leading to NVQ level 2 in food processing and cooking, and in professional cookery. There are no formal entry requirements. You can progress to an Advanced Apprenticeship.

Advanced Apprenticeships in hospitality and catering offer training leading to NVQ level 3 in professional cookery.

FOLLOW THESE STEPS TO BECOME A CHEF

1. Finish school with the best grades you can get, especially in any hospitality or food technology subjects offered at your school.

2. Work as a kitchen assistant — even part time — because it will give you invaluable experience in a commercial kitchen.

3. Complete an apprenticeship in the hospitality industry, as a kitchen assistant, a general trainee chef or a specialised pastry or baking chef.

4. Learn about the industry you have joined and its opportunities, and be prepared to develop your own palate by trying lots of new foods, ingredients and flavours.

5. Be prepared to work long hours, especially early in your career.

6. Do a course on running a small business if you want to set up your own restaurant, café or catering business.

7. Never stop learning! The secret to being a successful chef is always wanting to touch, taste and learn about food. The more you explore the world of food — how ingredients react to cooking and combine in different ways — the more confident you will become.

Contract catering

is one of the most rapidly expanding parts of the industry. They provide food for events and places like hospitals and schools. Catering firms recruit large numbers of qualified chefs and kitchen assistants. Some larger companies train their own staff.

Small-scale cooking

The opportunities here are normally in up-market situations. Jobs could involve preparing meals for private parties, yachts or executive dining rooms.

Specialist catering

Many people follow a vegetarian or other special diet and to cater for this, there are specialist courses available. Many of these courses are part-time.

DID YOU KNOW?

16- and 17-year-olds entering employment are entitled to paid time off during normal working hours for study or training if they do not have qualifications equivalent to five GCSEs at grades A*-C. Your Connexions/careers service will have more information.

OTHER RELATED CAREER AREAS TO CONSIDER:

Food and drink production
Bakery and confectionary
The meat industry
Food science and technology
Dietetics
Brewing and wine making

Is this for you?

Do you love food but are not sure that cooking is for you? There's a whole range of job options that involve food. You could consider a career in restaurant management, or sales for a catering company. Or you could become a restaurant consultant, or a food writer or stylist.

Food scientists and technologists consider the nutritional value, quality and safety of the food and drink we buy. They examine ingredients and work out what changes will occur during processing to alter the flavour and texture of the product. This is a challenging and fast-moving area of the industry.

Food and drink production

This includes all of the stages which turn raw ingredients into a finished, packaged product. Staff don't need particular qualifications but, when employed, they may be able to study for NVQs in food and drink manufacturing operations.

Glossary

broth — thin soup of meat, fish or vegetable stock

buffet — meal of several dishes where guests help themselves

catering — to provide, and sometimes serve, food

commercial kitchen — kitchen that prepares food for sale

cuisine — style of cooking

food technology — study of food production, handling and storage

garnish — something added to a dish for flavour or decoration

glaze — to make a surface shiny by putting a liquid substance (a glaze) onto it and leaving it or heating it until it dries

hospitality industry — industry that provides accommodation, food and beverages. It includes restaurants, bars, hotels, resorts, travel and tourism.

hygiene — degree to which people keep themselves or their surroundings clean, especially to prevent disease

molecule — simplest unit of a chemical substance, usually a group of two or more atoms

olfactory epithelium — lining of the spaces above and behind the nose in the middle of the face that contains receptors and nerves that provide the sense of smell

pasta — a food made from flour, water and sometimes egg

plating — act of arranging food on a plate

preheating — to heat an oven to a particular temperature before putting food in it

receptor — nerve ending that reacts to a change, such as heat or cold, in the body by sending a message to the central nervous system

recipe — set of instructions telling you how to prepare and cook food

special — dish that is available in a restaurant on a particular day

station — area where a person is assigned to work

stock — liquid in which meat, fish or vegetables is simmered for long periods

tastebud — taste receptor on the surface of the tongue

Useful contacts and websites

Contact your Connexions/careers service for information on jobs, local courses and work-based learning. You can obtain course prospectuses direct from colleges. In many large towns and cities, there are specialist catering employment agencies.

Information about various careers in the food and drink industries (including a virtual careers adviser called Dunkan) is available on *www.improveltd.co.uk*

Springboard UK – 3 Denmark Street, London WC2H 8LP. Tel: 020 7497 8654. *www.springboarduk.org.uk* Promotes hospitality, leisure, travel and tourism careers.

People 1st – 2nd Floor, Armstrong House, 38 Market Square, Uxbridge UB8 1LH. *www.people1st.co.uk* Tel: 0870 060 2550. The Sector Skills Council for the hospitality, leisure, travel and tourism industries.

Institute of Hospitality - Trinity Court, 34 West Street, Sutton, Surrey SM1 1SH. Tel: 020 8661 4900. *www.instituteofhospitality.org*

The Craft Guild of Chefs - 1 Victoria Parade, 331 Sandycombe Road, Richmond, Surrey TW9 3NB. Tel: 020 8948 3870. *www.craft-guild.org*

British Hospitality Association (BHA) - Queens House, 55-56 Lincoln's Inn Fields, London WC2A 3BH. Tel: 0207 404 7744. *www.bha.org.uk*

The BHA also publish an online directory of good employers - which can be found at: *www.bestpracticeforum.org*

Academy of Culinary Arts - 53 Cavendish Road, London SW12 0BL. Tel: 020 8673 6300. *www.academyofculinaryarts.org.uk*

The British Food Trust - No.1 Greenbank, Burleigh, Gloucester GL5 2PL. *www.greatbritishkitchen.co.uk*

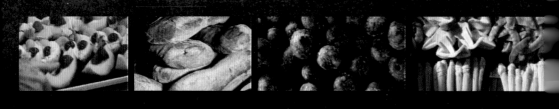

Index